JOSEPH MOORE

HELPING SKILLS

for the Nonprofessional Counselor

St. Anthony
Messenger
Press

CINCINNATI, OHI

Nihil Obstat: Rev. Edward J. Gratsch
Rev. Hilarion Kistner, O.F.M.

Imprimi Potest: Rev. John Bok, O.F.M.
Provincial

Imprimatur: +James H. Garland, V.G.
Archdiocese of Cincinnati
October 21, 1991

The *nihil obstat* and *imprimatur* are a declaration that a book is considered to be free from doctrinal or moral error. It is not implied that those who have granted the *nihil obstat* and *imprimatur* agree with the contents, opinions or statements expressed.

The term "wounded healer," used by Henri J.M. Nouwen in *The Wounded Healer: Ministry in Contemporary Society*, copyright ©1972 by Doubleday & Company, a division of Bantam, Doubleday, Dell Publishing Group, Inc., is used with permission.

The prayer by Mother Teresa, in *Words to Love by...*, copyright ©1983 by Ave Maria Press, is used with permission.

Cover design by Don Nesbitt
Book design by Julie Lonneman

ISBN 0-86716-174-4

Published by St. Anthony Messenger Press
Printed in the U.S.A.

Contents

Introduction 1

CHAPTER ONE
Theories of Helping 3

CHAPTER TWO
Physician, Heal Thyself 13

CHAPTER THREE
Building Helping Skills:
Nonverbal Communication 21

CHAPTER FOUR
Let's Look at Anger 31

CHAPTER FIVE
Questioning the Helpee 35

CHAPTER SIX
Crisis Intervention 41

CHAPTER SEVEN
Guiding a Group 55

CHAPTER EIGHT
Some Final Remarks:
Limitations of Rogers' Theory 59

AFTERWORD
The Example of Jesus 63

BIBLIOGRAPHY 65

Introduction

Many people today, because of their activities or positions in their parish communities, are counselors or helpers to others. Although the Church clergy do have training in counseling skills, many people don't necessarily turn to a priest or ordained minister for counseling. You may be a eucharistic minister, a catechist, a director of religious education, a youth minister, a youth group leader or peer minister, a sponsor in an RCIA program or maybe you're involved with separated or divorced people or a support group for the bereaved. In fact, sometimes it seems that we are sought out as counselors or helpers whenever we take on a role within the Church community.

To whom a person turns for help has more to do with who you, the helper, are than what you are. Research demonstrates that your personality characteristics are far more significant than the credentials or title you hold. People who are open and warm, nonjudgmental and caring, and who have the capacity to be good listeners are the ones sought out for help in the Christian community. That's why many of you reading this book find people coming to you for advice and counsel—you possess these admirable personality traits. So at the outset, relax and rejoice that someone perceives you to be a caring helper. Don't focus on skills you lack; those can be acquired through experience, training and reading books such as this one. It's much easier to acquire skills than personality traits, so begin your reading of this book with a positive feeling about yourself as potentially a very effective helper.

CHAPTER ONE

Theories of Helping

Many theories of counseling have developed since early in this century—theories about how human beings can find inner freedom, peace and happiness. The theories of Sigmund Freud, Austrian neurologist and founder of psychoanalysis, are among the earliest. One of his ideas is that freedom is found by recollecting early childhood memories to gain insight into why our personalities are shaped a particular way. Through psychoanalysis we can begin to understand our early experiences and freely choose our future.

Albert Ellis is the founder of rational-emotive therapy. Rational therapists, such as Ellis, believe our negative thoughts about ourselves keep us unhappy and unfree. What we tell ourselves about ourselves and others gets us into trouble—and can get us out of it. Hence, these therapists say we should substitute the self-defeating messages we tell ourselves (e.g., I am unattractive, unintelligent, of little worth and so on) with more rational statements so we can begin to make choices for a brighter future.

Behaviorism represents a pragmatic approach to

3

helping. Originated by B. F. Skinner, behaviorism uses behavior modification to reward (as a positive reinforcement) and punish (as a negative reinforcement) people for their actions. For example, emotionally disturbed children are given tokens for food at the school cafeteria if they behave (likewise, these same tokens would be withheld for unacceptable behavior). Skinner's theory emphasizes changing outer behavior first with positive (reward) or negative (punish) reinforcement in order to change inner feelings, as opposed to changing inner attitudes first.

Reality therapy was originated in 1957 by William Glasser, M.D., when he became dissatisfied with the traditional Freudian approach he was being taught as a resident psychiatrist. Basic to Glasser's theory is the individual person's responsibility to fulfill his or her basic needs without depriving others of the ability to fulfill their needs. Reality therapy in practice tries to get people to talk about the real issues in their everyday lives and those things they can do something about, accept that they are responsible for choosing their activities and then help them choose how they can improve their behavior in an effort to detach them from unhealthy, negative fixations or behaviors.

American psychologist Carl Rogers presents a nondirective, client-centered approach to helping people. It is his theory that we, as *nonprofessional* helpers, will follow.

There is truth and wisdom in every theory of therapy including those we have just reviewed and the many more we have not. Professional counselors with formal training are most often eclectic therapists. In

4

other words, they draw from all good theories and incorporate what appears to be helpful in each into their own approaches, although they may lean more strongly toward one theory or another.

For our purposes we are going to follow mostly Rogers' theory because it is easily accessible to nonprofessional helpers and because it does not put us at risk for counseling someone in the wrong direction. However, it may be valuable to you to study other approaches. If you feel so inclined, research other theories at your local library or bookstore and absorb various viewpoints aboout helping people find inner happiness.

Rogerian Counseling

Rogers' monumental work *Counseling and Psychotherapy*[1] explains his theory of helping, in which he emphasizes that clients must sort out issues for themselves rather than therapists giving specific direction to their clients. (Rather than use clinical terms like "client" or "patient" in this book, from this point on, we will call you the "helper" and the person who comes to you the "helpee.") Rogers' basic idea is that the helper is nondirective, that is, does not tell the helpee what to do or how to solve the problem. The helper's role is just to listen, although we really shouldn't say just to listen. Listening in Rogers' view is a helping skill requiring

---

[1]Rogers, Carl R., Ph.D. *Counseling and Psychotherapy*. Boston, Mass.: Houghton Mifflin Publishers, 1942.

5

much patience and practice. In our frantically-paced world, we know that listening, real listening, is a rare and beautiful gift we can give to each other.

A Christian Viewpoint

As we examine helping skills, keep in mind that ultimately for the Christian, inner peace and ultimate happiness are found in Jesus Christ. We can participate meaningfully in recovery groups and Twelve-Step programs like Alcoholics Anonymous, we can receive psychotherapy and become much happier and freer people, we can learn to be in touch with our feelings and be better communicators in our relationships.

But none of these approaches in and of themselves can bring us the same level of happiness and peace that belongs to those who are close to Jesus Christ. In other words, all psychotherapies only work to a point, can only promise a certain degree of liberation. We must be careful not to preach to our helpees—that is rarely ever appropriate. It's just as important for us as helpers, however, to always remember we are not saviors and that we can only help people to a certain degree—the rest is between them and God. As St. Augustine said in his *Confessions*, our hearts *are* restless until they find rest in God. One of the reasons so much unhappiness prevails in our culture is precisely because so many people live lives unconnected to Christ.

In order to help people connect to Christ, you might, at some point in counseling, suggest that they turn to prayer, receive the Sacrament of the Eucharist,

6

the Sacrament of Reconciliation, read the Scriptures or join in a eucharistic community. But make these suggestions gently and only at a point where you feel that such remarks would further a person's healing. Your own caring is the best reflection of Jesus Christ that a helpee can have. Reflect upon this beautiful prayer by Mother Teresa:

Dear Jesus,
Help us to spread your fragrance everywhere we go.
Flood our souls with your spirit and life.
Penetrate and possess our whole being so utterly
    that our lives may be a radiance of yours.
Shine through us
and be so in us
that every soul we come in contact with
    may feel your presence in our soul.
Let them look up and see no longer us
but only Jesus.
Stay with us
and then we shall begin to shine as you shine,
so to shine as to be light to others.
The light, O Jesus, will be all from you.
None of it will be ours.
It will be your shining on others through us.
Let us thus praise you in the way you love best
    by shining on those around us.
Let us preach without preaching,
    not by words but by our example,
    by the catching force
    the sympathetic influence of what we do
    the evident fullness of the love our hearts bear to you.
Amen.[2]

---

[2]Mother Teresa. *Words to Love By....* Notre Dame, Ind.: Ave Maria Press, 1983, p. 47.

7

Listening Versus Advising

Jean came to me experiencing marital distress and admitted she was ambivalent about separating from her husband. This was her second marriage and she didn't want to admit failure twice. She was also tied financially to her spouse by joint ownership of their home and by paying tuition to private colleges for the education of their two sons. And yet the love between them had died and he, in fact, had been involved with another woman for several years now. She asked me what she should do.

The most tempting response for any of us is to give advice. And yet this is the *least* helpful response we can make. Good helpers refrain from advice giving because it simply is unhelpful. The attitude helpers need, according to Rogers, is "unconditional positive regard." Let's explore what he means. People need:

1) to talk to someone so they can

2) get in touch with their feelings so they can

3) make choices for their own happiness.

If I, the helper, tell Jean what to do, then I am making several mistakes. First of all, I am cutting short the whole process where she talks out her confusion to get in touch with her "heart." I am also robbing her of the chance to take ownership of her life choices. And lastly, I am taking responsibility for a choice that is not properly mine. Suppose I give her advice and the solution I suggest does not work out—who is to blame then?

When I get a request for advice, I treat it as if

8

someone tossed me a basketball which I gently toss back.

Helpee: "What do you think I should do?"

Helper: "I'm really not sure."

Helpee: "Well, do you think I should...?"

Helper: "I can't answer that for you."

Helpee: "Well, if you were me, what would *you* do?"

Helper: "Well, I'm not you and our complexities as people are so different we really can't project choices onto each other."

Helpee: "So you're saying you really can't help me."

Helper: "No, I'm saying the answer lies within you, but right now it's buried beneath a lot of confusion. I think if you can talk to me more about it, you will find the answer you so desperately seek."

It takes discipline to resist giving advice. But we need to realize that people don't really want advice even though they may appear to request it. Think about a time you took a problem to a friend or helper. Were you really wanting advice or were you looking for a little sympathy or encouragement, affirmation of a choice toward which you were leaning, or were you needing to talk out the problem to someone?

As caring people (and you are a caring person if you are reading this book), we may have rescue fantasies—we want to take away the hurt and make people "all better." But the old adage rings eternally true: The only way *out* of pain is *through* it. The ambivalence,

9

the agonizing, the fear and insecurity of making the wrong choice—all these need to be "walked through" if a person is to come to a deep interior decision for which she or he takes full responsibility. I want to empathize as a helper, which means I want to try to stand in the other person's pain to imagine what it must be like to have this particular struggle. But I simultaneously want to realize that as much as I may care for and about this individual, I cannot remove the suffering with my advice, I cannot help the person sort out the hurting feelings.

Most of us are confused about our feelings and have difficulty sorting them out. We are often more in touch with our intellects than our emotions. Did you ever try to make a decision by listing on a piece of paper all the reasons for and against a certain choice? It usually isn't a very useful exercise. Why? Because it ignores our feelings and is an attempt to base choices on reason alone. My helpee, Jean, may list twenty reasons why she should stay in her marriage and only three why she should leave, and yet her gut, or heart, may be pulling her in a powerful way toward divorce. As Blaise Pascal, the French mathematician and philosopher, said: "The heart has its reasons, which reason does not know."[3]

Therefore, Jean needs to talk out her confusion and ambivalence about what to do; she doesn't need me telling her what to do. This talking out may take one meeting with me, but more likely it will take several—or it may even take a year or two! Jean needs to get in touch with the deepest desires of her heart which will in turn

---

[3]Blaise Pascal from *Pensées*, 1670. Reprinted in *The World Treasury of Religious Quotations*. Ed. by Ralph L. Woods. New York, N.Y.: Hawthorn Books, Inc., Publishers, 1966, p. 424.

lead her to the freedom that comes from making a decision for herself. Right now she is caught in a web of indecision. As she talks out with me all the pros and cons of her situation—all her doubts and fears, all her shame and hopes—she will eventually get in touch with what she needs to do for her own happiness. It is by this talking to a good listener that we can connect to and trust our deepest feelings.

The next step is decisionmaking. It will take time for the person to muster the strength and courage to do what must be done or to accept what must be accepted. That's why I said that Jean and I may need to meet over many months before she makes a real choice. Now this doesn't mean that lengthy therapy is typical—in fact, it isn't for the nonprofessional helper. Most of your helping will probably be short term with specific goals in sight. If long-term help is needed, you will probably want to refer the individual to a professional counselor who has expertise in the area of concern. In the case of Jean, I might want to refer either her or her and her husband to a marriage counselor.

Finally, you must understand that it is easier to be a listener and not an advice-giver when you're not an intimate friend of the helpee. For example, if Jean were my sister I would probably have strong feelings about the choices before her. Maybe I would detest her husband and advise her to leave him. That's why it's far easier to counsel acquaintances than close friends or family members. We are much less capable of objectivity when we are closely bound emotionally to the helpee. That doesn't mean that we can't use our helping skills when people close to us present a problem, but it does mean that we need to be realistic about how subjective we might be in a particular situation. Sometimes our role should be simply to refer our friend to a professional counselor or, at least, someone less emotionally involved in the situation.

CHAPTER TWO

Physician, Heal Thyself

Before we talk more about developing specific helping skills, let's discuss what the experience of counseling another does for and to us. It is primarily a chance for us to grow. People who study to become professional counselors usually experience psychotherapy themselves as a part of their curriculum. We need to understand human nature in general by understanding ourselves in particular.

While we are unique creatures, there is a universality to our needs, desires and psychological suffering/happiness. If I know what makes *me* tick, I can help others more effectively. If I'm out of touch with my own self, I am also out of touch with others. If I can accept my own humanity and sexuality with all my weaknesses, neuroses and areas of un-freedom, I am more able to accept other weak human beings.

This is why the helping relationship can be so challenging—I am forced to address the same issues within myself which others are speaking about to me. If Jean is talking to me about her reasons for wanting a divorce, that discussion might challenge me to reexamine my own marriage or other relationships.

13

Henri Nouwen, the spiritual writer, calls the minister a "wounded healer."[4] The way we heal each other is by sharing our pain and our struggles. By mutually confessing our failures and weaknesses, doubts and fears we paradoxically gain strength for the journey of life from each other. In other words, the helper isn't someone superior to the helpee, but rather a fellow traveler on the same road looking for the same things: happiness and freedom.

Barbara Varenhorst, the pioneer of peer counseling among youth in the United States, says one lesson we derive from the Good Samaritan story in Luke 10:29-37 is that former victims make the best helpers.[5] Because the Samaritan was a persecuted person he could more quickly relate to the plight of the wounded man in the road. If we are in touch with our own pain and incompleteness, we can quickly relate to the pain of others, even if it is from a source different from ours.

Sometimes, however, we are too close to our helpee's problem to be effective. For example, the winter my father died of a brain tumor I was approached by a client who was coming to terms with terminal cancer in his parent. I was not able to discuss my concern because I was still dealing with my own grief issues. I simply told this client that the tragedy in my life was too fresh and my feelings were too raw to be able to discuss this topic—and then I referred him to someone else. Today,

[4]Nouwen, Henri J.M. *The Wounded Healer: Ministry in Contemporary Society.* Garden City, N.Y.: Doubleday & Company, Inc., a division of Bantam, Doubleday, Dell Publishing Group, Inc., 1972.

[5]Varenhorst, Barbara. *Training Teenagers for Peer Ministry.* Loveland, Colo.: Group Publishing, 1988, p. 28.

since several years have now passed since my father's death, I would welcome the client who presents the problem of a terminally-ill parent. In fact, I think that because I have been through a similar episode and have a perspective derived from time's healing, I am probably the ideal helper for such a person to approach.

'Judge ye not!'

Another challenge to helping another is to avoid being judgmental. Now there is a difference between being judgmental and making judgments. We all make judgments constantly—what we like and don't like, how we spend or don't spend our time, what we do and don't do. Our judgments are based upon our tastes, our preferences, our priorities, our values, our moral code and our Christian faith. We cannot help but to be constantly making judgments!

But to be *judgmental* is to set ourselves up as a sort of review board of the attitudes and actions of others. To be judgmental is to presume that we know another person's motivations, limitations, psychological make-up and moral capacity. To make judgments is acceptable and natural; to be judgmental is unacceptable for both the counselor and the Christian. Look to Jesus who was the least judgmental person to walk the earth. He seemed to be always hanging out with the rejected and marginalized people of Jewish and non-Jewish society. Consider the woman being stoned to death for adultery. Jesus makes a judgments because he tells her to go and sin no more. However, he is at the same time

15

nonjudgmental because he doesn't look down upon her or condemn her. He accepts her and then challenges her to change.

As a helper we will hear things that perhaps shock or disgust us or depart from our own morals or value systems. We may hear about rape or incest, physical or sexual abuse, abortion, homosexuality or drug use. We may be told about suicide attempts or tales of deceit or violence. While we can't help being surprised or even shocked, we can learn to not verbalize or express these emotions, which may appear as judgments.

I'll never forget the time Ronnie, a sixteen-year-old girl in my church, asked me if the church youth group could take up a collection to pay for her abortion. Neither will I forget the day my cousin confessed to me that he had been a drug addict for five years. These conversations really surprised me, but I tried to remain as calm and nonchalant as I could, lest my reaction of shock and surprise be misconstrued as judgmental. I, of course, made interior judgments that abortion and drug addiction are opposed to the life-giving values of my Christian faith. But I did not look down upon these individuals or condemn them to a category of bad person in my own posture toward them.

The older I get, the more in touch with my own humanness I am and the more I listen to the life stories of others, the less judgmental I am. As the ancient philosopher Terence said, "I am a man; and nothing human is foreign to me."[6] I may not have the same set of

---

[6]Terence from *Heautontimoroumeno I.i.* Reprinted in *Dictionary of Quotations.* Collected and arranged and with comments by Bergan Evans. New York, N.Y.: Delacorte Press, 1968, p. 329.

16

issues or behaviors as other people, but I recognize that the same vulnerability from which their actions spring also resides in me. I, too, am *capable* of hatred, abusing others as well as myself and taking shortcuts to human fulfillment (e.g., drug abuse, sexual promiscuity, other "quick fixes"). I find that the more I can face my weaknesses, the more I can tolerate others' weaknesses. I recognize that the same fundamental longings within my heart are in the hearts of all men and women. And I think about the calm and open character of Jesus who never seemed jarred by the weaknesses of others. Peter denied him three times and Jesus could forgive and accept.

So if someone, like Ronnie, presents a problem on which I may have strong moral convictions I must ask myself if I am capable of being objective with this person and her problem. If I were sexually abused as a child, am I capable of listening to a helpee who has sexually abused his own children? Again, am I too close to this issue emotionally to be helpful? Or if I was never abused but feel a moral outrage against child abuse, am I able to listen to a helpee who has this problem, listen to the person nonjudgmentally and with compassion?

First, I must accept that this person's moral values may not be similar to mine and that by talking out her confusion with me she may make a choice contrary to my views. Then, I can follow two paths in my counseling of this person. Usually, I try to challenge myself to be open to helping this person with the problem. The pain, shame and reasons underlying the person's behavior most often bring me from the mountain of judgment to a place of humility, the place where I feel Jesus stands.

17

Occasionally, however (and it is rare), someone will present an issue to me about which I have such a strong opposing moral view that I feel it will be impossible to be objective and nonjudgmental. In that case, I simply am honest with the helpee and tell the person that I am not the best person to discuss that topic and I try to refer the helpee to someone who can be more open than myself.

The Challenge

Hence, we are challenged by Christ's example in our ministry to accept people on real terms—be they our terms or not.

My colleague Tom is a Jesuit priest who is the chaplain of an AIDS clinic in a large metropolitan hospital. He was invited to give a workshop for chaplains and other caregivers a few years ago at the international AIDS conference. Tom decided to ask one of his most animated patients a question. Rufus was a black man, almost forty years old, who had been an intravenous drug user and lived on the streets most of his life. He was then in the final stages of AIDS, confined to a hospital bed and dying. Tom explained he was going to the conference and might not see Rufus alive again. But, Tom told Rufus, he wanted the main point of his presentation to be advice from Rufus, a client whose honesty and perceptiveness Tom had come to appreciate. So he asked him, "Rufus, if you could give just one word of advice to all the chaplains and caregivers in the world working with AIDS patients, what would that advice be?"

18

Rufus clasped Tom's hand, looked up at him with eyes glazed with tears and said: "Just tell them to be real, man, just tell them to be real."

CHAPTER THREE

Building Helping Skills: Nonverbal Communication

We recognize today that much of our communication is without words. We have learned, for example, to interpret immediately many facial expressions of our friends, spouses and family members. When they are hostile, sad or exuberant, we can often detect these emotions by their nonverbal cues without them telling us how they feel. We will soon be discussing how as helpers we need to look for these feelings in our helpees. But first we need to study how our own body language sends messages to our helpees as to whether or not we are listening and concerned.

Active Listening

Here are five tips for good listening:

1) Look the helpee in the eye. Don't stare the person down, but don't look away since that action conveys disinterest. The helpee may need the strength of your eyes for encouragement to keep

talking. This is especially true if you are in a group setting with other people present.

2) If you are seated, lean forward slightly toward the helpee. Active listening, as Carl Rogers calls it, is a chore, a task. It is not merely to listen well but *also to let your helpee know that you are listening.* If you slouch back in your chair, it may again convey an attitude of disinterest.

3) Respond to what is being said with an occasional nod of the head and/or an utterance such as "uh-huh" or "sure" or "mmm"—those signal words reassure people very subtly that they are indeed being heard.

4) Keep your facial expressions consistent, attempting not to register shock or surprise, disgust or judgment, ridicule or cynicism. A simple look of interest is best.

5) Refrain from little annoying habits which may distract the helpee. These might be things such as smoking, twisting your ear, doodling or tapping a pencil. I sometimes find myself stroking my beard, and when I discover I'm doing it, I stop immediately.

Try also to *listen* for the feelings beneath the words. A person may say to you: "No, I'm not depressed" or "I'm not upset" or "I'm not angry at her," and yet the very tone of his voice and the way he appears to you (his "affect," as therapists call it) may suggest the opposite. My advice is to trust your gut instinct about how the person is feeling (especially if you already know the person) and probe a little bit even if he is in a sort of denial. People are often unaware of how they really feel, which is why they need to talk to someone like you—to get in touch with their actual emotions.

Ask clarifying questions to let people know you are "with them" as they speak. "You mean he really said that?" "Is this the first time you had met her?" "So you feel strongly about this?" Remarks and questions that don't interrupt the helpee but pepper the dialogue at certain points reassure helpees that you are really absorbing what they have to say.

Focusing Attention

In our world of haste one of the most beautiful gifts we can give to each other is undivided attention. So many people today ache with emotional pain partly because they feel no one has bothered to listen to them or to try to understand them. A good helper makes a valiant attempt to block out all other interferences when a helpee approaches. If you keep having side conversations with passersby, answering the telephone, continuing to do some task or even allowing your mind to wander to all the tasks you need to accomplish that day, you are sending messages to the helpee that you really aren't all that interested in what she has to say.

Indeed, I would say that occasionally the helper is presented with the additional task of keeping the helpee focused on what she has to say. Sometimes people start to reveal a problem and go off on a tangent that clouds the conversation. I remember a young woman telling me about all the friction between her and her mother. She was confused about how to structure a family celebration at Christmas because of this conflict. But she got sidetracked by talking all about how famously her husband got along with *his* mother and how they enjoyed visiting her in the summertime and what activities they did on their vacation with her. I found myself faced with the task of helping her refocus our conversation by saying gently: "But you were talking about your own mother—it sounds like there are some issues to be resolved if you're going to enjoy the holidays, aren't there?"

I think people go off on tangents in conversations for two reasons. Some people just have less linear minds that don't approach reality in linear A, B, C steps. These people are not less logical. They just take a different approach in their thought processes, pausing to flirt with detail and enjoy an immersion in what seems peripheral to another person but in their reality has a bearing on what is being said. Some people go off on tangents in self-defense. Sometimes we open up to others about a private or perhaps embarrassing problem and immediately after we open up we become scared that we have ventured into this territory. So rather than explore these scary or perhaps painful feelings, we find it more comfortable, less threatening, to talk about some minor point which, we hope, will distract us and the person listening to us. But a problem-solving conversation does need to retain focus, and so if a person's verbalization tends to wander, you should refocus the helpee's attention. An astute helper will recognize the wandering behavior for what it is.

More Responding Skills

We have discussed several basic ways to respond to helpees nonverbally and by showing understanding with brief remarks or questions. But the responding skill requires more. As helpers, we function as mirrors in which the helpee can see a reflection of himself. How? The helpee takes this jumble of confused or painful feelings from within and attempts to put them into words. By this attempt at verbalization he is exposing the problem for you to see. When you function as an active listener you are giving him the chance to listen to his own words and you, in a sense, reflect his problem back at him just as a mirror reflects a person's image. And when the issues get reflected back they are seen with more clarity. Helpees need this clarity in order to make their life choices.

Sometimes a person is so confused she says to me: "I'd like to talk with you about this, but I don't know where to begin." I tell her to start anywhere, that it really doesn't matter where she begins the story. But I also say that if she doesn't ever begin, if she never tries to put this jumble of feelings into words for another human being to hear, then she will never be able to clearly see what it is she needs to do. The "stiff upper lip" theory that says I can go off by myself to a woodland retreat and solve my own problems within my own psyche without the benefit of a caring listener is a seriously misguided viewpoint.

Once the helpee has told you his story, summarize what he has said. This succinct response again lets the speaker know that you are listening *carefully* to what is being said; it also helps him clarify the issues involved, which is the goal of the helping relationship, and it also helps keep the helpee from going off on a tangent. You can summarize:

1) the *content* of what has been said or

2) the *underlying feelings* in what has been said.

Here's an example: The first response summarizes the content; the second, the underlying feelings.

Helpee: "I woke up at 4:00 this morning and couldn't get back to sleep. So I got up around 5:00 only to discover that my dog had torn his ear outside during the night so I rushed him to the vet. This made me late for work and my boss wasn't very understanding. And on top of all this, I had forgotten to bring a lunch so I had to go hungry all day."

Response #1 (content summary): "Sounds like you've had a really tough day."

Response #2 (feeling summary): "You must feel pretty frustrated after a day like that."

Here's another example of the two response types:

Helpee: "I like both of the colleges where I was accepted. One has the exact major I want, but I got a better financial package at the other one. My

26

parents aren't pressuring me to go to one or the other, but my best friend is because she was accepted at one of them."

Response #1 (content summary): "So you're faced with a difficult choice because both places have advantages."

Response #2 (feeling summary): "You must be pretty confused about what to decide."

Can you see how in the second response the feelings are the focus, whereas the first is a summation of what has been presented or how you have heard the problem? Both are helpful ways of responding. The feeling summary, however, is the more significant of the two responses because it connects folks to what is going on inside them. Remember, I said people are often out of touch with how they really feel even though it becomes obvious to you in conversation with them. If you observe hostility, frustration, anger, sadness, despair, exuberance or anticipation of impending happiness—indeed, any range of feeling—you definitely want to express to the helpee this observation with a feeling summary at some point in the conversation.

It takes a bit of listening before you feel comfortable reflecting back to a person the feeling or feelings you hear. You could practice making the two types of responses with a friend, asking her to give you a "paragraph of problems."

Here are some ways content and feeling response summaries could begin:

"So you're saying that...."

27

"Sounds like you're feeling...."

"In other words, you...."

"What I'm hearing you say is...."

"Then to put it simply, the problem is...."

Again you can see how you are acting as a mirror, reflecting the issue back to the helpee.

Our society does not always respect feelings. We put a high priority on reason and often in our childhood, our feelings are belittled. As children we may be taught that feeling impatience, anger or hostility is bad and ought not to be expressed in any way by "good" little boys or girls. Those of us who are male may have been taught to suppress certain fears or feelings of tenderness as "unmasculine." Some people believe Christianity prohibits the expression of certain negative feelings such as anger or hatred. We often deny, distort or repress our feelings, being afraid to admit them to ourselves, let alone to others. It's this hiding of feelings from our own selves that is the root of much of our emotional confusion and anxiety.

As a helper, you might label a feeling inaccurately; this mistake is OK. For example, you might say, "You seem pretty jealous," and the helpee might answer you, "Well, I think I'm more hurt than jealous." Or you might say, "Sounds like you're pretty depressed," and the helpee might say, "No, I'm not really depressed. I think I'm just discouraged." You see, in correcting your summary the helpee is further clarifying her feelings to herself. That's why labeling a feeling mistakenly is just as helpful as labeling it correctly. So don't agonize over the correctness of your observation, just take a risk and name what you hear or think you hear. Of course, sometimes helpees also disown accurate labeling of feelings, which is part of their problem, to be sure.

Indeed, if you label a feeling, try to pinpoint it as accurately as you can. There are many nuances or shades of meaning to feeling words. For example, each of the following words' meanings differs slightly, although each group refers to the same fundamental human emotion.

anger:	fear:	sadness:	joy:
furious	dread	depressed	exuberant
peeved	anxious	"bummed out"	upbeat
explosive	terrified	desolate	"excellent"
"ticked off"	nervous	"down in the dumps"	glad

You might want to take a minute and think of how many other words you know which fall into these four basic categories. Again, it helps to try to label an observed feeling with the word or words that come closest to it.

CHAPTER FOUR

Let's Look at Anger

We stated earlier that, in counseling, the helper grows as the helpee does. Since many Christians have difficulty with anger, let's examine ourselves in relation to it. What we need to realize with respect to *all* feelings that scan the human landscape is that emotions in and of themselves are neither right nor wrong—feelings have no morality. If I feel hateful, jealous or revengeful, I simply have feelings and would do well to admit them, at least to myself. It's what I do with the feelings that can be right or wrong and where morality comes into play. Acting or not acting on emotions is not the same thing as acknowledging or not acknowledging their existence within me.

Very often as little children we are punished and reprimanded for our anger. Anger often accompanies a child's punishment for bad behavior and little children can confuse the two, i.e., which behavior is "bad": the act they performed or the anger they are exhibiting as a result of being punished. And so many of us grow up feeling it is bad to be angry or we feel guilty when we are angry. Some of us try to repress our anger; this repression causes depression. It is unfortunate that polite society doesn't accept anger as a legitimate human emotion that needs appropriate expression. We confuse a person's anger with us with the issue of whether or not she likes us.

As a helper you may need to deal with the anger of a helpee. Therefore, it is important that you can cope with your own feelings of anger if you are going to be able to accept this emotion in someone else. Use the following test to help you determine how well or poorly you deal with your own anger.

Anger Test

Answer yes or no to the following questions.

1) Can you admit to yourself and others that you are angry?

2) Do you express your anger to the person at whom it is intended?

3) Do you refuse to sulk or nurse grudges?

4) Do you express yourself right away when angered rather than let your anger build over time into an explosion?

5) Can you express your ideas calmly if they differ from the ideas of others?

6) Can you refrain from hitting someone when you are angry at him?

7) Do you think it is OK for a Christian to show anger?

8) Do you feel that anger is a normal human emotion?

9) Can you let go of any guilty feelings after you have expressed justified anger?

10) Is depression an infrequent experience in your life?

If you have answered "no" to one or more of these questions, you may have a problem with the appropriate expression of anger.

To deal with anger within yourself, follow these basic rules to emotional health:

1) Admit to yourself that you *are* angry; this honesty is crucial.

2) Express your anger in a reasonable manner at the time it is felt.

3) Try to express the anger to the person with whom you are angry; if this is impossible, express it to a third party or alleviate the emotion by physical activity, like going for a long run or scrubbing the bathroom floor or whatever activity provides an outlet for you.

4) Let go of the anger after it is expressed; don't indulge yourself in dwelling on hurt feelings.

5) Negotiate solutions to problems where you and the other party are willing to both give and take.

In your counseling, remember that many people think anger is wrong or un-Christian or impolite. You can help the person by naming anger when you observe it in her. You can tell her that anger can be expressed reasonably and appropriately and that a person can learn this life skill if she is willing to take a few risks. You can teach her it is healthy to express anger because repression leads to a delayed explosion of pent-up anger or, more commonly, depression.

We know today that chronic depression can be caused by a chemical imbalance and can be treated with medication. (See Chapter Six for more details on helping a person who is suffering from depression.) But more commonly when people feel depressed and cannot name the source of this general feeling, it is because they have not dealt properly with feelings of anger. Anger that is repressed, denied and turned inward generates feelings of depression. This is yet one more reason why it is so important for people to be able to accept and deal with this crucial human emotion.

CHAPTER FIVE

Questioning the Helpee

Questioning is indeed an art—that is, questioning in a helpful way. One good reason to question is to gather information. It will be difficult to respond if you lack a developed portrait of your helpee's problem. You need the background information surrounding a presenting problem. If, for example, someone wants to discuss the prospect of divorce with you, you will need to know a little about the history of the relationship. If someone says: "My mother's boyfriend really gives me the creeps when he comes over to our house. I can't wait until he's gone," you are going to need more explicit details to even understand what the helpee means. You will have to ask: "What do you mean, 'he gives you the creeps'?" "Well, he always wants to sit next to me." You will *still* need to probe further about his behavior until you have a clear picture of what the helpee is trying to say.

Information-gathering questions are appropriate and helpful to the point where they provide you with the necessary picture of the problem. They become inappropriate when asked out of curiosity and not out of a need to know. For example, questions about the

35

boyfriend like "What kind of a car does he drive?" or "Does he have hair on his chest?" or any other probe which simply entertains me would not be helpful at all and definitely would undermine the trust level of the conversation for the helpee.

Furthermore, avoid asking "why" questions. This word in itself requires the speaker to explain something. To have to explain is to defend, often to the point of justifying. This tendency is especially so when "why" questions are asked in succession.

Open and Closed Questions

A closed question is a question which the helpee can respond to with a simple "yes" or "no." It may be asked to gather facts, but it isn't very helpful. For example, if you ask the helpee "Do you still love your husband?" it sets her up to only respond with a "yes" or "no." It would be better to phrase the question in such a way that the helpee is invited to elaborate on the issue. For example, "Can you tell me more about your feelings for your husband?" or "How would you describe your feelings for each other?"

The role of the helper is fundamentally to get the person in need to verbalize the problem (especially the feelings beneath the problem). And questions are the most concrete way to get people to open up. Good questions really get the helpee to express the problem to you and simultaneously to himself. They also help the helpee probe the feelings he has, which he may be unaware of.

36

Six 'Don'ts' for Good Helpers

Once the person you are counseling opens up and begins to discuss her problems, be cautious in your responses to her. You should try to avoid the following six conversational bad habits.

1) *Don't talk too much about yourself.* Sometimes when we can identify with someone's problems (for example, he is dealing with an alcoholic spouse and you have also dealt with alcoholism in your family), we want to share our experience and let the person know what worked for us. While it is good to state that you can relate to a problem through personal experience, it isn't helpful to elaborate when the other is seeking your assistance. Make your identifying remarks, but keep them brief and immediately swing the spotlight back onto your helpee.

2) *Don't turn off the person's emotions.* If someone discusses an issue with you and verbally (and nonverbally) expresses emotions such as joy, anger, sorrow or weeping, don't tell the individual to restrain the expression. Let her yell, let him sob, let the teenager jump for joy. Our reaction is more a commentary on how well or poorly we accept in ourselves these same feelings we are witnessing in the other.

3) *Don't attempt to comfort with clichés.* When we don't know what to say to a helpee, we can be

37

tempted to respond with clichés: "Tomorrow's another day," "There are more fish in the sea," "Things take time," "This too shall pass," "Time heals all wounds" and so on. These remarks tend to dismiss the problem as not worth your effort. They can also make the helpee feel as though you really didn't hear what she was trying to say. And perhaps more significantly, these tired clichés send the message that the person really ought not to feel as she does.

4) *Don't offer sympathy*. Helpers are there for support but more so to assist in seeking out solutions. Friends can provide sympathy. It isn't helpful to simply commiserate with someone and hold his hand. Be sensitive and understanding, but prod the helpee toward the future and decisions.

5) *Don't warn*. Again, you are not a moral judge. Don't paint scenarios of what it will be like if she does or doesn't take certain courses of action—let a helpee articulate those things for herself through open-ended questions: e.g., "So what will you do if you leave the house: where will you go?"

6) *Don't lecture or blame*. Do not ascribe blame to either your helpee or to some other party, and surely don't preach a little sermon to the person. Again, you are there to listen so that the helpee can make needed decisions for future happiness, even if it's simply to accept more peacefully a painful reality.

Our temptation in these six "don'ts" is basically to be a problem solver. Rather, we are to be nondirective most of the time, making statements like: "Did you ever consider...?" We need to avoid remarks such as "You should," "If I were you I'd" and "What you need to do is." It is not our role to analyze the problem. It is the helpee's job to do that by putting the issues into words. Our task is to be good listeners. And, as you're probably realizing by now, effective listening is a real skill requiring both practice and a good dose of self-discipline.

CHAPTER SIX

Crisis Intervention

Now, for the moment, forget everything we have said about being a nondirective helper! Most of what we have discussed applies to life situations where there is time and leisure to talk things out. But a crisis is a different matter. Let's define a crisis as an event (or a series of events with a cumulative impact— the proverbial "straw that broke the camel's back") in which a person's psychological balance is thrown off and normal methods of coping with life's difficulties no longer work—for example, when talking to a friend, praying or running around the block doesn't alleviate the stress of the situation.

When confronted with a crisis the helper's task is often to function as a referral agency—to get the person the needed help. If it is a stabbing, mugging, rape or drug overdose, I would take the person to an emergency room, or perhaps a rape crisis intervention center or a shelter for battered women. Or, if it's a suicide attempt, I would first get medical help. Here are some basic steps for a helper to follow in a crisis:

41

1) *Assess what happened.* A correct perception of what has happened will assist you in taking action. If the helpee has been victimized, it is very helpful for her to tell you what happened. Why? Because victims feel powerless and vulnerable. The first step toward regaining power is being able to name what has occurred.

2) *Do the first thing that needs to be done.* This might be to go to a hospital, call the police, call the person's parents or spouse or stop the bleeding.

3) *Remain calm.* Stabilize the crisis by keeping your own emotional reaction to it contained.

4) *Refer.* Get the person the appropriate psychological help after the crisis (e.g., rape counselor, suicide counselor, drug rehabilitation program and so on). Even if the helpee will not seek out the help right away, you can at least provide the referral. It's a good idea to already know what agencies and services exist locally so you are prepared for times of crisis.

Specific Critical Issues

Rape. Most rape victims are young women and many of them know their attackers. In fact, date rape is unfortunately quite common in our culture—which, simply put, means forcing one's date to have sex. The shame that is attached to the person's feelings of victimization makes this crisis a particularly difficult one. It takes some people many years to recuperate in a psychological sense. As a nonprofessional helper I suggest that you, of course, be nonjudgmental, encourage any small signs of the victim's attempt to regain power over her life and refer her to a support group, therapist or agency that specializes in this issue.

Grieving and Loss. There are different experiences of loss in our lives: losing a job, moving to a new place, seeing our teenager move away to college. Any loss brings change. All loss brings a particular type of grieving and the struggle to adapt to life anew. In many senses life is a train ride with constantly changing scenery. Yet many of us would prefer to cling endlessly to one snapshot or scene along the way. Life *is* change. As a helper, your role is to help the person accept the change.

The most profound form of loss is, of course, the death of someone we have loved: a parent, a spouse, a child, a close friend. Loss of a spouse is the most stressful, according to psychiatrists Thomas H. Holmes and Richard Rahe of the University of Washington School of Medicine, who researched stress for twenty years.

As helpers there really isn't much we can do for the grieving person except to be there as a support, literally, a shoulder to cry on. Indeed, the fundamental goal in helping grieving people is to allow them to just be. Try to realize that the person will be going through various stages in the grief process and that there is no appropriate time frame in which this grieving ought to

43

occur. It is a great fallacy to believe that intense grief ought to be dealt with in one year and that a person should then "get on with life." There is no appropriate time period, but for many people it is much longer than a year. Again, allow the person to be. If he wants to dwell on stories about his deceased wife, let him. In other words, encourage the person in whatever he says he needs rather than acting out of your own projections of what he *should* need.

Sexual Abuse. Unfortunately sexual abuse is a common phenomenon in our culture. A sexual abuser of children is usually a trusted adult. Hence, the shame and fear associated with this experience tends to make the child very secretive. If a young person speaks to you about being abused, first of all believe the person. Don't make judgments and refer the individual immediately to appropriate help. Because the emotional scars of sexual abuse are so destructive and permanent, the victim is in need of long-term therapy. And, if a perpetrator confides in you, remain nonjudgmental of this psychological illness and get the person to professional help immediately.

Terminal Illness. If you are helping someone cope with a terminal illness, recognize that people progress through certain specific stages during their illness. They don't necessarily go through them in order, i.e., stage one first, then stage two and so on, but they definitely do experience an inner journey of feeling from denial to acceptance.

Elizabeth Kübler-Ross has researched these stages

in her pivotal book, *On Death and Dying*.[7] She suggests that at first the diagnosis is too overwhelming and so we deny it. Then we move into bargaining (usually with God) over the illness, e.g., "Take away this cancer and I'll give all my money to the poor." Then when we let go of bargaining, we feel anger followed by resignation or a feeling of giving in. If we reach the final stage, acceptance, we move to where we can find inner peace. The loved ones of the dying person are also going through stages similar to those of the patient. As helpers, we can simply "be there" as a support to these people and allow them to be anywhere on the spectrum from denial to acceptance. If they want to cry and reminisce with us, that's OK. It's a question of not reacting out of our need to deny, to be a rescuer or to cheer up sick people. Our supportive presence is in itself sufficient comfort.

Coping With AIDS. Persons with this particular terminal illness are coping not only with a debilitating disease but also with society's prejudice toward AIDS patients. They may perhaps expose sexual behaviors or drug addiction by contracting AIDS, which may further compound negative attitudes toward them. Persons with AIDS are in need of a great deal of support and understanding. As helpers associated with the Church we can remind these people as well as all of society that our hero, model and savior, Jesus, usually associated himself with those rejected by the Jewish culture of his

---

[7]Kübler-Ross, Elizabeth. *On Death and Dying*. New York, N.Y.: Macmillan, 1969.

45

day. By standing with AIDS patients we remind everybody of Jesus' radical love of all men and women. Again, we may have personal moral convictions that are opposed to certain behaviors which have led to the HIV infection, but we are not judgmental in our interactions with these people. The families of AIDS patients also require care and support. My suggestion would be to refer both AIDS patients and those who love them to the growing number of support groups for those who share this mutual struggle for wellness and dignity.

Divorce. Next to the death of a spouse, Holmes and Rahe reported divorce as the most stressful and traumatic of experiences. So many painful feelings are involved in divorce, such as betrayal, loneliness and failure. The amicable divorce is rare indeed. There may be also feelings of shame and guilt for Christians with a sacramental perspective of marriage. Children of divorcing parents often feel guilty of having caused the crisis (irrational though these feelings may be), a false sense of hope that the crisis is only temporary and feelings of being divided in terms of loyalty. Divorce is indeed a painful road for all whose lives are touched by it. As a helper you can offer support and encouragement, companionship in lonely times and the promise that healing is ultimately on the horizon.

Eating Disorders. Eating disorders generally impact young women in our culture, although males are susceptible also. Surveys in the United States indicate that more than ten percent of girls between ages thirteen to eighteen are afflicted with anorexia nervosa or

46

bulimia—a very staggering statistic when you consider that probably even more girls are suffering in view of the secrecy that usually surrounds these behaviors.

Bulimia is a disorder involving compulsive overeating followed by self-induced vomiting, use of laxatives or arduous exercise to get rid of the same food. Anorexia nervosa is a disorder where a person refuses to eat and has a distorted view of her own size or figure. Our consumer society upholds the slender female figure as the ideal of beauty. A young woman who feels unaccepted, out of place, without friends and so on, may choose to alleviate her painful feelings by aspiring to achieve the prerequisite slim figure of the ideal woman.

Many people alternate between these two disorders. Because these diseases are life-threatening, early intervention is important. People with eating disorders require both medical and psychological help. When you suspect an eating disorder, be aggressive in your questioning of the helpee and refer the person to the appropriate help. For more information, contact the American Anorexia/Bulimia Association, Inc., or the National Association of Anorexia Nervosa and Associated Disorders, whose addresses and telephone numbers are listed in the bibliography on page 65.

Illness and Physical Disability. When listening to a sick person share his fears about an illness, don't operate out of your own fears or your need to rescue another person from inevitable pain. If his apprehensions are imagined or not rooted in truth, then, of course, you want to direct the person toward reality. But if his fears have a basis in truth, then it is a

47

tremendous comfort for him to share them with someone who can listen to and accept them.

If you are helping a person adjust to a permanent disability, you need to realize that she will need to go through stages similar to those experienced by a person learning to accept a terminal illness. Attempts to cheer up a physically disabled person are not usually helpful. What does help, again, is to be a good listener. Neither pretend that the disability doesn't exist by trivializing it nor focus your pity on the disability exclusively. A physical handicap gives a person opportunity to grow spiritually and psychologically.

Suicide. Many myths surround suicide. The first one is that you could plant the idea in a person's mind who had not previously considered it. Not true! If someone is very depressed and you suspect him of being suicidal, ask him. No harm done. Another myth is that if a person is determined to die, he can't be stopped. Not so! He is probably very ambivalent about what to do. Suicidal people don't really want to die—they just want the pain to stop. A third myth is that people who talk about suicide won't really do it. Eight out of ten suicide victims have given warnings in one way or another—often these warnings are very indirect, which is another barrier to proper diagnosis.

If you determine a person is suicidal, then the next step is to ask her the plan. The more concrete the plan, the more dangerous the situation. Don't allow yourself to be sworn to secrecy. It's better to risk a friendship by breaking confidentiality than it is to lose a friend to death. Besides, consider yourself—bearing a secret of suicide is a tremendous burden which you should not carry alone.

If the person is presently at risk, she shouldn't be left alone. If it's a young person, the parents and those who live with this teenager need to be told. Seek help aggressively for this individual. This action in itself demonstrates to the person how much you care for her. Statistically, in our society, females make more suicide attempts than males. Males, however, succeed more often in suicide because they choose more lethal means. When dealing with teenagers, recognize that their suicidal ideations are usually unrealistic (for example, imagining people's remarks at their own wakes which, of course, they will never really hear) and that many such deaths among adolescents occur under the influence of alcohol or other drugs.

Depression. The first agenda in helping a depressed person is to observe if there is an immediate cause for the feelings. If so, the depression is a quite normal reaction to recent stress and, probably, is not long lasting. However, if the depression is more chronic, less definable and less traceable, I would refer the person to a physician. We know today that depression can be caused by disturbances in the chemistry of the brain and certain medications can alleviate the disorder. This is a first step in diagnosing a depression that hangs on.

Recall my earlier remarks about anger. Repressed anger, hostilities never ventilated, can lead to depression. Many people cope with hurt and anger in this way. These people need to talk out their feelings in the classical Rogerian way described earlier. You may be

49

the person for the job. Whenever you feel that the person's psychological problems are too profound, however, too much for you to handle or be helpful with, suggest that the individual seek professional help. If she doesn't, your alternatives are: (a) to continue to be a helper nonetheless, (b) say that you cannot help anymore since the issues are beyond your capacity or (c) consult with a professional yourself as to how you ought to proceed with this helpee.

A footnote on abortion: In 1985, 1,588,550 abortions were performed in the United States. Jesus would probably be as outspoken in his condemnation of abortion in our own day as he was of the money changers in the temple in his day. Jesus was not silent when he took a strong moral stand. At the same time that he condemned the sin, however, he would not condemn the sinner. Jesus' compassion and his capacity to both forgive and challenge in the face of human weakness offers us the example we need in every difficult issue we face when dealing with the struggles of others. Because abortion is so prevalent in our society, there is a tremendous need for Christian helpers who can accept these women (and sometimes males who have encouraged the abortion) in a nonjudgmental way. Depression often accompanies the guilt and self-hatred that many times affect these people after the abortion; these feelings must be worked through patiently.

Abortion is a tough issue at the level of the individual, writes Archbishop Daniel E. Pilarczyk in *Twelve Tough Issues: What the Church Teaches—and Why*. He says that sometimes the decision to get an abortion "is made in panic and desperation. That does not make it a right

50

decision, of course, but it reminds us that Christian love and compassion are not offered only to those who have never made a wrong choice."[8]

In your counseling of people who have had abortions, remind them it is healthy to feel guilty for wrongdoing and to feel guilty when we act selfishly. But teach them that the purpose of guilt is to produce change, to help make new pledges for tomorrow. Encourage them to seek reconciliation with the Church after resolutions are made. You will notice in your work with people that many of us choose to wallow in guilty feelings rather than to accept the challenge of inner change. Your task as a helper is to bring the person to meet that inner challenge.

Alcoholism and Other Addictions. Our culture has been called the "addictive society." We are more aware of dysfunctional families and the impact of this dysfunction on future generations. We recognize addictions are among us. One classic addiction that has been with us for many years is alcoholism. After much study and observation, we have learned about both its painful effects and the road to recovery. Some people who abuse alcohol or other drugs are able to stop with a simple resolution and others with one-on-one counseling. The majority of addicts, however, need the support of a group struggling together. The first step in any addiction is to admit the problem. Denial among addicts is incredible and often lasts for many years until

---

[8]Pilarczyk, Daniel E., Archbishop. *Twelve Tough Issues: What the Church Teaches—and Why.* Cincinnati, Ohio: St. Anthony Messenger Press, 1988, p. 11.

the addict hits rock bottom in some way or other. It isn't necessary to wait for intervention until then—the earlier, in fact, the better. Alcoholics Anonymous (AA) offers a twelve-step recovery program for people who want to end their addictions by reliance on a "higher power" (or God) and one another.

But if the addict doesn't respond to intervention, those impacted by his behavior ought to take stock of their own needs. Groups exist for family members affected by the person's addiction. Al-Anon and Al-Ateen are wonderful support systems for family members that offer helpful guidance in resisting enabling behaviors. Al-Anon is a twelve-step program for the families of addicted people. Al-Ateen is a support group for children dealing with a parent's alcoholism or older sibling. Adult Children of Alcoholics (ACOA) meets to heal the pain of adults who suffered emotional damage growing up in homes in which alcoholism was present. This growing awareness of the alcoholism's effects on family members' behavior patterns in adulthood has been extremely therapeutic for thousands.

Narcotics Anonymous (NA) is a support group following a twelve-step theory similar to AA for persons addicted to drugs. (Nar-Anon provides support for family members of these addicts.) OA is for overeaters, GA is for gamblers, DA is for people with credit and debt dependencies and SA (Sex Addicts Anonymous) and SLAA (Sex and Love Addicts Anonymous) are for people with sexual addictions and patterns of unhealthy love relationships. Confidentiality is crucial to the success of these support groups; mutual respect and trust are hallmarks of their meetings. They are excellent referral

52

sources for pastoral ministers confronted with addiction or co-dependency in their ministry. Each group's local chapter provides directions for meeting places and times.

So many of us are healed by sharing the stories of our struggles to be both human and holy. We can do this in one-on-one sharing or in groups such as we have just discussed. The important point here is to encourage people not to keep their pain and problems locked within themselves but to open up to others who are caring members of the Christian community or other communities to which they belong.

CHAPTER SEVEN

Guiding a Group

You may sometimes be a group discussion leader or facilitator, or perhaps be part of a common discussion of a mutual problem. Let me offer some guidelines about leading a group, which you can apply to fit your particular situation or role.

1) If everyone in the group is not comfortable with each other or does not know each other, ask each person in turn to say his or her name (or some other information). You may even wish to initiate an ice-breaking activity or engage the group in informal conversation before the formal discussion begins. It helps a group when members are relaxed and unafraid to share.

2) If moments of silence do occur, don't be afraid of them and immediately rescue the group by talking yourself. Silence can be very creative and can pressure (in a healthy way) group members to speak.

3) Allow group members who prefer to be silent and

not share just to be. They may be gaining much by listening. Encouraging participation is fine and drawing out shy people with open questions is a skill. But never pressure a person to speak.

4) Allow yourself to be dethroned. In other words, if the group begins to work without your leadership, allow it to be. A group that can function on its own is the sign of successful leadership.

5) If one person dominates the group's conversation, you as the leader have the responsibility to intervene and move the discussion to others.

6) Allow others to share more than you do. Your task as a leader is to provide a setting in which others can speak.

7) Don't be afraid of the expression of emotion in the group; if someone becomes upset and starts to cry, a gentle human touch may be appropriate.

8) It is helpful for groups to adhere to time frames limiting discussion. You will notice that psychotherapists generally set a fifty- to sixty-minute limit to counseling sessions. One reason for this is to allow the client enough time to speak, but not an endless amount of time. We often need the pressure of a time frame to encourage us to get out what we have to say. And many times clients (unfortunately) wait until the last five minutes to share what is truly troubling them. This can also

be the case with groups. If group members feel that they have all the time in the world to discuss, they may never collectively focus themselves enough to accomplish the task. As a leader you may also need to remind the group to move away from irrelevant discussions and return to the focus of the meeting.

CHAPTER EIGHT

Some Final Remarks: Limitations of Rogers' Theory

Carl Rogers' nondirective, client-centered approach is immensely valuable to people such as ourselves who are often thrust into healing relationships with very little background in counseling skills. It provides a framework and an atmosphere where others can unburden themselves through verbalizing to us and in that process discover solutions within their own hearts. This is indeed a very healing experience.

Criticism of the Rogerian technique is twofold. First of all, some would maintain that it is not goal-oriented enough and can encourage long-term dependency on the helper. In other words, since the person verbalizes his problem and gets in touch with his feelings does he then move on to make decisions in his life or does he remain stuck? By being stuck I mean, does the helpee simply continue to discuss the problem again and again without any resolution?

As a helper you can recognize that this is not a healthy situation for either you or the helpee, in which case you have two options. One is to move the person toward specific decisionmaking/practical goals. The other is to say that you can no longer be of help and that he ought to choose another helper or seek professional counseling.

This recommendation doesn't presume a person doesn't need time before she can act. I remember Jane who came to talk with me about her relationship with her husband. It took her six months before she had the courage and inner strength to call a lawyer. But I had a sense as we talked that year that she was building her inner resources and moving almost imperceptibly toward a brave decision regarding her unfaithful husband. But let's say she wanted to come to me for a second and third year and bemoan her spouse's infidelity. I would then feel that our conversations were not helpful and perhaps even served as a substitute or excuse for not taking action. Each case requires individual judgment in which you have to follow your instincts. I usually get a gut feeling about whether or not a series of conversations are helping the person progress in any direction or not. I suspect you will get this feeling too; my suggestion is just to trust your instincts in the matter.

The other weakness in the Rogerian approach is that at times not enough anxiety or creative energy is generated within the helpee to urge that person toward change. The consequences of this energy deficit are similar to the lack of goals we have just discussed and so the alternatives for the helper are similar. Try to get the helpee to think of incentives that would motivate him to take action. For example, if you were counseling Jane, ask her what her life would be like if she were not married to her husband. Her fantasizing or daydreaming along these lines may provide that needed spark of creative energy to generate change.

In summary, remember you should never get so aligned with a theory of counseling that you forsake common sense and your gut instincts. As I said in Chapter One, most professional therapists are eclectic in their approach, borrowing what they consider best from all the various schools of counseling and fashioning them into their unique approach. The art of helping is a definite skill that requires practice. The more you find yourself thrust into helping relationships, the more you will find yourself growing in this art. Since reading is also a wonderful way to enhance your helping skills, I have provided a brief bibliography to encourage your self-education (see page 65).

The Example of Jesus

Brother Roger Schutz, founder of the interdenominational and ecumenical Protestant monastic order at Taizé, has said that watching a person who stays and prays in church alone for a few minutes after the rest of the congregation has departed teaches more about faith than any words or sermon. In a parallel way, the care and compassion you exhibit as a person does more for human helping than all the degrees of psychiatry and psychology. I hope you feel more adequate, not less, after reading this little book. Rather than focusing on all the counseling theories you haven't even studied, take stock of all the life experiences you have had as well as the human qualities you possess which you bring to a helping relationship.

It would be unfair to stretch the Scriptures and say that they give us a clear model of Jesus as the ideal therapist. But there are two aspects of his relationships with people that I feel do give us an idea of his approach. The first, to reiterate, is his nonjudgmental stance. Think of his conversations with the woman at the well, the woman caught in adultery and with Peter who denied him. Jesus ate with tax collectors and chatted with lepers, blind people and others looked down upon by Jewish society. The other characteristic I notice when I read the Gospel is that Jesus so often asks people what it is they need. He helped Simon's mother-in-law only after he was asked to intervene and then cured her because of her faith (Luke 4:38-39); he healed the leper who bowed before him and trusted in him (Luke 5:12-14). How quick we are today to advise without first asking the person's need and then listening. Good listening is rare in our day. Some have suggested that is why so many of us pray—in essence, we have a captive listener. Hear Jesus' answer to Martha that she frets and worries too much while her sister Mary sits at his feet and *listens* (Luke 10:41-42).

Because the process of inner healing is within the other person, as helpers we need constantly to turn over this healing to Jesus. Some helpers are comfortable sharing prayer out loud with the helpee. This can be a beautiful moment if both helper and helpee are comfortable with this prayer form. But we can also pray privately in our own way for helpees. As we said at the outset, the skills and process of helping another can assist in bringing a person to a certain point of coping, growth or change. But beyond our necessary and noble human efforts, we need to turn over the struggles within ourselves and within others to the Spirit of God who also dwells in us all.

BIBLIOGRAPHY

Further Reading for Nonprofessional Helpers

American Anorexia/Bulimia Association, Inc., 133 Cedar Lane, Teaneck, NJ 07666, (201) 836-1800.

Auer, Mary Glynn, Elmer Fischesser and Roberta Tenbrink. *Redemptive Listening: A Communication Workshop for Every Christian.* Audiocassette. Cincinnati, Ohio: St. Anthony Messenger Press, 1988.

Bodo, Murray, O.F.M., and Susan Saint Sing. *The Desert Speaks: A Journey of Prayer for the Discouraged.* Audiocassette. Cincinnati, Ohio: St. Anthony Messenger Press, 1984.

Conroy, Maureen, R.S.M., Thomas Klee, Rea McDonnell, S.S.N.D., and Rachel Callahan, C.S.C. *Spirituality and the Addictive Personality.* Audiocassette. Cincinnati, Ohio: St. Anthony Messenger Press, 1989.

Johnson, Richard, Ph.D. *A Christian's Guide to Mental Wellness*. Ligouri, Mo.: Ligourian Publications, 1990.

Harkaway, Jill Elka. *Eating Disorders*. The Family Therapy Collections. Rockville, Md.: Aspen Publications, 1987.

Hazelden Educational Materials, Pleasant Valley Road, Box 176, Center City, MN 55012, 1-800-328-9000 (for informational booklets on eating disorders).

Kennedy, Eugene. *Crisis Counseling: The Essential Guide for Nonprofessional Counselors*. New York, N.Y.: Continuum, 1981.

May, Gerald, M.D. *Addiction and Grace*. San Francisco, Calif.: Harper, 1988.

Moore, Joseph. *A Teen's Guide to Ministry*. Ligouri, Mo.: Liguorian Publications, 1988.

_____. *When a Teenager Chooses You—As Friend, Confidante, Confirmation Sponsor: Practical Advice for Any Adult*. Cincinnati, Ohio: St. Anthony Messenger Press, 1989.

Murphy, Kathleen, O.P., and Maurice Proulx, M.S. *A Workshop in Spiritual Direction*. Audiocassette. Cincinnati, Ohio: St. Anthony Messenger Press, 1991.

National Association of Anorexia Nervosa and Associated Disorders, Box 7, Highland Park, IL 60035, (312) 831-3438.

Nisbet, Jim. *Avoiding Burnout in Parish Ministries*.

Audiocassette. Cincinnati, Ohio: St. Anthony Messenger Press, 1991.

Nordby, Vernon J., and Calvin S. Hall. *A Guide to Psychologists and Their Concepts.* San Francisco, Calif.: W. H. Freeman and Co., 1974.

Nouwen, Henri J. M. *The Wounded Healer: Ministry in Contemporary Society.* New York, N.Y.: Image (Doubleday & Co., Inc.), 1979.

Rohr, Richard, O.F.M. *Breathing Under Water: Spirituality and the 12 Steps.* Audiocassette. Cincinnati, Ohio: St. Anthony Messenger Press, 1989.

Sheehan, Barbara, S.P. *Caring for God's People: Meeting Critical Pastoral Needs.* Audiocassette. Cincinnati, Ohio: St. Anthony Messenger Press, 1990.

Stone, J. David, and Larry Keefauver. *Friend to Friend: How You Can Help a Friend Through a Problem.* Loveland, Colo.: Group Books, 1983.

Turpin, Joanne. *Jesus' Journey, Our Journey: A Way of the Cross for the Sick and Shut-In.* Cincinnati, Ohio: St. Anthony Messenger Press, 1987 (also available as an audiocassette).